CELEBRATE AUSTRALIA

SHARE THE SPIRIT

PROUDLY MADE IN AUSTRALIA

KEN DUNCAN
PANOGRAPHS®

The Sydney 2000 Olympic Games will be characterised by the vibrant qualities of Australia itself and the visionary hope felt at the turn of a new millennium. They will reflect the vitality, spontaneity, good humour and good nature of Australia.

The Mark of the Sydney 2000 Olympic Games echoes the sails of the Sydney Opera House, and the inspirational qualities of the Olympic torch. At the centre stands the athlete—the hero of the Games. The boomerang flies toward 2000 as a symbol of the Olympic athlete's skill.

The colours of the Sydney 2000 logo represent the elements—water (blue), earth (yellow) and air (red), which are also the colours of the Australian landscape. The Olympic symbol consists of the five Olympic rings and represents the union of the five continents and the meeting of athletes from throughout the world at the Olympic Games.

TITLE PAGE
Millaa Millaa Falls, Queensland

LEFT
Refuge Cove, Victoria

Australia's treasure lies in its superb natural heritage. In the red-dust deserts of the Outback, or under the lush green rainforest canopy of the north, we are close to the heart of this great continent. Australia is still a frontier land, where people can walk amid pristine wilderness and actually feel its power and majesty.

The natural world casts a wonderful light on our lives. When we spend time reflecting on the beauty of creation, we are better able to put things in perspective. Nature forces us to realise that our own lives are truly small in comparison to the universe.

Earth is our ship and we have a responsibility to look after it. We are linked with the land—it nourishes our souls.

DEDICATION
This book is dedicated to the most special person in my life, my wife Pamela.

PREVIOUS PAGE
Dimond Gorge, Western Australia

LEFT
Natural Arch, Queensland

PREVIOUS PAGE
Sunrise, Kata Tjuta, a culturally significant area to Aboriginal people

RIGHT
The Twelve Apostles, Victoria

NEXT PAGE
On the road to Gundagai, New South Wales

The areas pictured on this and the previous page are normally inaccessible to the public. In both cases, special permission was granted to photograph these spectacular scenes.

PREVIOUS PAGE
Russell Falls, Tasmania

RIGHT
*Forgotten Dreams, Burra, South
Australia*

NEXT PAGE
Koolewong, New South Wales

ABOVE
The Arch, Purnululu National Park, Western Australia

NEXT PAGE
Mossman Gorge, Queensland

The wilderness is a place of stillness. A wilderness area that hasn't been brought under human control has a presence which is phenomenal. It's a place of stillness which touches your inner being.

Such places are sanctuaries where we can be restored. All people need to be recharged from time to time in the midst of their busy lives. Wilderness invigorates us and creates freshness; it fills us with beauty, bringing forth new life.

Walking through a wilderness area is like walking through an ancient world. Little has changed in thousands of years. There is a timelessness about wild places that strengthens us.

As we approach the dawn of a new millennium, we need to protect our age-old sanctuaries, both for ourselves and for future generations.

LEFT
Walls of Jerusalem National Park, Tasmania

NEXT PAGE
Country church, Mullengandra, New South Wales

PREVIOUS PAGE
Sunset over the Twelve Apostles,
Victoria

LEFT
The Remarkables, South Australia

NEXT PAGE
Jim Jim Falls, Northern Territory

PREVIOUS PAGE
Hopetoun Falls, Victoria

RIGHT
Uriala Valley, New South Wales

ABOVE
Normanton Railway Station, Queensland

ABOVE
Richmond Bridge, Tasmania

NEXT PAGE
Sunburnt country, Flinders Ranges, South Australia

Lying on an Australian beach you know you're close to paradise. This island-continent has nearly 20,000 kilometres of coastline, with so many beaches that many of the most beautiful have never been named.

Australia is a country where water, earth and air reach perfect unity. Light binds them together— sun-drenched, shimmering, crystal light falling from a blue sky that goes on forever.

Ours is truly a land of wide open spaces. Sitting on the white sand of this beach that seems a million miles from anywhere, gazing out across the vast expanse of turquoise ocean, there's nothing to interrupt the horizon as far as the eye can see.

RIGHT
Cape Leveque, Western Australia

NEXT PAGE
Rising Force, Terrigal, New South Wales

PREVIOUS PAGE
Haast's Bluff, Northern Territory

LEFT
*Fan palms, Cape Tribulation,
Queensland*

NEXT PAGE
The Labyrinth, Tasmania

PREVIOUS PAGE
Reflections, Ellery Creek, Northern Territory

ABOVE
Paradise, Whitehaven Beach, Queensland

ABOVE
The Pinnacles, Western Australia

NEXT PAGE
Uluru, Northern Territory, World Heritage listed for both its cultural and natural significance

RIGHT
Tidal River Beach, Victoria

NEXT PAGE
Ebor Falls, New South Wales

ABOVE
King George Falls, Western Australia

ABOVE
Island Arch, Port Campbell, Victoria

Perched high in the Great Dividing Range, a traditional slab hut looks out over a vast mountain wonderland. Drawing their materials direct from the land, early Australian settlers carved out a place for themselves in an environment of harsh beauty that called forth their deepest devotion.

Australia's history is a tale of human courage and determination. From the Aboriginal people who lived for thousands of years in gracious harmony with the land, to the white pioneers who staked everything on their hopes for a better life, Australia has always called forth great dreams.

RIGHT
Craig's Hut, Alpine National Park, Victoria

NEXT PAGE
Desert landscape, Kata Tjuta, Northern Territory

PREVIOUS PAGE
Snow gums, Victoria

LEFT
*The Three Sisters, Katoomba,
New South Wales*

**CELEBRATE AUSTRALIA -
SHARE THE SPIRIT**

First published in 1998
by Ken Duncan Panographs® Pty Limited
ACN 050 235 606
P.O. Box 3015, Wamberal NSW 2260,
Australia. Telephone: (02) 4367 6777.
www.kenduncan.com

Copyright photography and text:
© Ken Duncan 1998.
Designed by Good Catch Design.
Edited by Owen Salter.
Colour separations by Purescript.
Printed by The Pot Still Press.
Bound by The Bindery.
Distributed by Gary Allen Pty Limited.

The National Library of Australia
Cataloguing-in-Publication entry:
Duncan, Ken
Celebrate Australia; a new millenium
ISBN 0 9586681 9 1.
1. Australia - Pictorial works. I. Title.
994.00222

TM©SOCOG 1996
http://socog.olympic.com.au